Wisconsin
The Badger State

Marcia Amidon Lusted

PowerKiDS press
New York

For my parents, Richard and Eleanor Amidon, with love

Published in 2010 by The Rosen Publishing Group, Inc.
29 East 21st Street, New York, NY 10010

First Edition

Editor: Nicole Pristash
Book Design: Greg Tucker
Photo Researcher: Jessica Gerweck

Photo Credits: Cover, p. 22 (bird), 22 (flower) Shutterstock.com; p. 5 Paul Damien/Getty Images; p. 7 © North Wind/North Wind Picture Archives; p. 9 © Layne Kennedy/Corbis; p. 11 © Robert Pickett/Corbis; p. 13 © Macduff Everton/Corbis; pp. 15, 19, 22 (Frank Lloyd Wright and Devin Harris) Getty Images; p. 17 © Richard Hamilton Smith/Corbis; p. 22 (Laura Ingalls Wilder) © Bettmann/Corbis; p. 22 (tree) © www.istockphoto.com/Greg Nicholas; p. 22 (animal) © www.istockphoto.com/John Pitcher; p. 22 (flag) © www.istockphoto.com/Dave Willman.

Library of Congress Cataloging-in-Publication Data

Lusted, Marcia Amidon.
  Wisconsin : the Badger State / Marcia Amidon Lusted. — 1st ed.
      p. cm. — (Our amazing states)
  Includes index.
  ISBN 978-1-4042-8120-2 (library binding) — ISBN 978-1-4358-3366-1 (pbk.) — ISBN 978-1-4358-3367-8 (6-pack)
  1. Wisconsin—Juvenile literature. I. Title.
  F581.3.L87 2010
  977.5—dc22
                                                2009002634

Manufactured in the United States of America

Contents

America's Dairy Land

In which state can you find the world's biggest **carousel**, a four-story building shaped like a giant fish, and enough cows to produce a year's supply of milk for more than 40 million people? The answer is Wisconsin!

You can find Wisconsin in the upper midwestern part of the United States. Wisconsin is shaped a little like a mitten. The top of Wisconsin touches Lake Superior. A tiny thumb-shaped **peninsula** sticks into Lake Michigan. The Mississippi River runs along the western edge of the state. Wisconsin is called America's dairy land because it produces so much butter, milk, and cheese.

This is one of the 15,000 dairy farms in Wisconsin. Each farm produces about 18,850 pounds (8,550 kg) of milk each year.

Native Past

Wisconsin gets its name from a Native American word, *ouisconsin*. *Ouisconsin* means "gathering of the waters." Native Americans, such as the Chippewas and the Oneidas, were Wisconsin's first people.

In 1634, a Frenchman named Jean Nicolet explored Wisconsin. France wanted the **area** because it was rich in animals with valuable furs and other helpful **resources**. In 1763, France gave Wisconsin to the British, in the Treaty of Paris.

After the American Revolution, the British gave up their claim on the land. The area then became a **territory** of the United States. Wisconsin became America's thirtieth state in 1848.

This painting shows explorer Jean Nicolet meeting Native Americans when he landed on the Wisconsin shore in 1634.

Rocks and Water

Wisconsin is known for its valleys, in which there is rich soil useful for farming. The state also has hills and rocky mountains.

Lakes and rivers are plentiful in Wisconsin. The Fox River is one of the only rivers in the country that flows north! Wisconsin also has hundreds of miles (km) of shore along Lake Michigan and Lake Superior. Tall cliffs and sea caves are found there.

In the south, Wisconsin's **climate** brings hot summers and mild winters. In the north, winters are colder. The state generally gets about 30 inches (76 cm) of rain every year.

This man is exploring the rocky shore of Lake Superior in a boat called a kayak. Many boaters visit the sea caves and cliffs that are found there.

The Badger State

Wisconsin is home to many different plants and animals. Grasslands there are filled with flowers like purple coneflowers and lupines. Maple trees grow everywhere. Thick pine forests draw hikers.

The state has animals such as white-tailed deer, beavers, swans, and wild turkeys. Large fish such as the muskellunge, or muskie, are favorites of many fishermen.

Wisconsin is known as the Badger State. The nickname comes not only from the small, furry badgers that live there but also from the men who mined Wisconsin's hills for lead. The men often spent the winter under ground, just as badgers do.

Here you can see a badger digging a hole in the ground that it will use for shelter. Its hole is also called a burrow.

What's Made in Wisconsin?

Many different things are made in the state of Wisconsin. Farmers in Wisconsin grow crops such as corn and hay. Some farmers also raise cows for beef. Wisconsin, though, is best known for making cheese. Most farms in Wisconsin are dairy farms. Dairy farmers raise cows for producing milk and milk **products**. These tasty products are shipped all over the country.

Other Wisconsin products include honey and ginseng. Ginseng is an **herb** that is used in cooking and in drugs. Fruits such as apples, strawberries, and cherries are also grown there. Vegetables grown in Wisconsin include snap beans, carrots, and green peas.

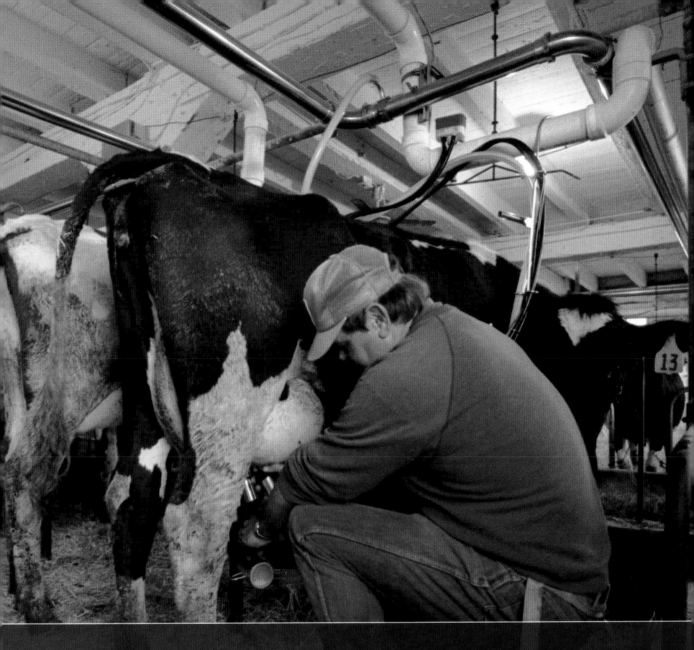

This farmer is milking a cow. It takes 10 pounds (4.5 kg), or a little more than 1 gallon (4 l), of milk to make 1 pound (.5 kg) of cheese.

More than Just Farms

Although Wisconsin has many farms, it also has factories. Wisconsin's factories make gasoline **engines**, X-ray machines, and machines that are used for mining and building homes and businesses. The state's factories also make parts for many of the cars and trucks we see every day. Wisconsin is home to one of the world's largest makers of **motorcycles**, Harley-Davidson, too. The first Harley-Davidson factory was found in the city of Milwaukee.

Nature plays a part in the goods that Wisconsin produces. The forests found in the northern part of the state supply trees that are used for making paper and other wood products.

This man is riding a Harley-Davidson motorcycle in a parade in Milwaukee. Harley-Davidson has been making motorcycles for over 100 years.

A Visit to Madison

Wisconsin's capital is Madison, which is found in the southern part of the state. Madison has more than 200,000 people living there. The people who live there come from many **diverse** parts of the world, such as Poland, Scandinavia, and Asia.

There are many cool places to visit in Madison. Madison has more than 260 parks and five nearby lakes. People can walk, swim, and sail there.

The Vilas Park Zoo and the Madison Children's Museum are fun places for kids to visit. The Overture Center offers storytellers and puppet shows. The Olbrich Conservatory has an indoor **tropical** garden.

The Wisconsin state capitol building, shown here, was built between 1906 and 1917. It cost $7.25 million to build.

Land of the Cheeseheads

Many people think of cheese when they think of Wisconsin. The state makes more cheese than any other state in the country. Many of Wisconsin's early farmers were from Europe, where they learned to make cheese. The farmers kept making cheese in their new homes.

Today, most Wisconsin cheese is made in factories. The Chalet Cheese Co-op is the only cheese factory in the country that makes a very smelly type of cheese called Limburger. Fans of Wisconsin's pro football team, the Green Bay Packers, are called cheeseheads. They wear special hats made to look like blocks of cheese!

Here you can see a young Green Bay Packers fan wearing a cheesehead hat at a game at Lambeau Field, in Green Bay.

Exploring Wisconsin

Wisconsin has something to offer everyone. You can go inside a four-story-tall **model** of a muskie fish at the Freshwater Fishing Hall of Fame. You can hop on the world's largest carousel in Spring Green.

For people who like the outdoors, there are many state parks all over Wisconsin. Hiking, swimming, and boating are only some of things you can do there. Wisconsin has auto races, too.

Many people visit Wisconsin to enjoy its beauty and the fun things that the state offers. Others think it is a wonderful place to live. Either way, Wisconsin has more than just cheese!

Glossary

area (ER-ee-uh) A certain space or place.

carousel (ker-uh-SEL) A park ride with toy horses that go around on a platform.

climate (KLY-mit) The kind of weather a certain place has.

diverse (dy-VERS) Different.

engines (EN-jinz) Machines inside cars or airplanes that make the car or airplane move.

herb (ERB) A plant used as a drug or for seasoning food.

model (MAH-dul) A copy of something, generally bigger or smaller than the real thing.

motorcycles (MOH-tur-sy-kelz) Two-wheeled machines on which people ride.

peninsula (peh-NIN-suh-luh) An area of land surrounded by water on three sides.

products (PRAH-dukts) Things that are produced.

resources (REE-sors-ez) Things found in nature that can be used or sold, such as coal or wool.

territory (TER-uh-tor-ee) Land that is controlled by a person or a group of people.

tropical (TRAH-puh-kul) Having to do with the warm parts of Earth that are near the equator. The equator is the imaginary line around Earth that parts it into two parts, northern and southern.

Wisconsin State Symbols

State Tree
Sugar Maple

State Animal
Badger

State Flag

State Bird
Robin

State Flower
Wood Violet

State Seal

Famous People from Wisconsin

Laura Ingalls Wilder
(1867–1957)
Born in Pepin, WI
Writer

Frank Lloyd Wright
(1867–1959)
Born in
Richland Center, WI
Architect

Devin Harris
(1983–)
Born in Milwaukee, WI
Basketball Player

22

Wisconsin State Map

Lake Superior

○ Superior

○ Ashland

Chequamegon National Forest

Nicolet National Forest

Wisconsin River

St. Croix River

○ Eau Claire

Green Bay ○

○ Appleton

Petenwell Lake

Lake Winnebago

Castle Rock Lake

Fox River

Mississippi River

Lake Michigan

Milwaukee ○

Madison ★

Racine ○

Wisconsin State Facts

Population: About 5,363,675

Area: 54,154 square miles (140, 258 sq km)

Motto: "Forward"

Song: "On, Wisconsin!" music by William T. Purdy, words by Judge Charles D. Rosa and J. S. Hubbard

Index

Web Sites

Due to the changing nature of Internet links, PowerKids Press has developed an online list of Web sites related to the subject of this book. This site is updated regularly. Please use this link to access the list:

www.powerkidslinks.com/amst/wi/